AuthorHouse™
1663 Liberty Drive
Bloomington, IN 47403
www.authorhouse.com
Phone: 1 (800) 839-8640

Published by AuthorHouse 04/04/2019

ISBN: 978-1-7283-0720-6 (sc)
ISBN: 978-1-7283-0721-3 (hc)
ISBN: 978-1-7283-0719-0 (e)

Library of Congress Control Number: 2019903993

authorHOUSE®

Acknowledgments

Jim and Louise Brainard enabled publication of Thunder Paws and the Snowboard through their most generous donations. They wanted to see the story in print because of their school aged grandchildren.

Appreciation to Steamboat's Alpine Bank, Rotary Club, City Market and Anti Bullying Communications Inc. for helping with printing costs of Thunder Paws and the Snowboard.

Barbara Coloroso international bullying expert and author of the bully the bullied and the bystander mentored Carpenter in structuring a story dealing with school bullying.

Lisa Lorenz Executive Director of Yampa Valley Autism Program thank you for asking me to write about a child who has autism.

Editorial help provided by Grace,

Robyn, Jim Brainard, Matt Eidt, Rob Carpenter, Buddy Dow, Gail Smith, Chase Bailey and Ms. Lewis' third grade students of Strawberry Park Elementary School Steamboat Springs Colorado. Thanks to their school principal Tracy Stoddard office manager Barb Hurley and educators including art teacher Erin Kreis and her students.

For teaching me about the layout of a children's picture book Michelle Sommerville is appreciated.

Peggy Axtell, Geoff Petis, Nancy Fryer, Lois Horowitz, Danielle Felici, Rose Ashes, Steamboat Springs Police Officer Kiel Petkoff, Dr. Neil and Joan Ganz, Mike Diemer, Roger Reynolds are thanked for their encouragement and enthusiasm.

Heartfelt appreciation to my husband Rob for always believing in my work and helping enable my dreams to soar.

"Wholey woofin' dog poop I smell mean behavior," thought service dog Thunder Paws as

William ran away with Abigail's snowboard.

Liam looked at Abigail and proclaimed, "William's a bully!"

"William's a bully, William's a bully, William's a bully," Abigail flapped her hands and exclaimed

loudly.

Thunder Paws gently nudged Abigail's arm with his nose then licked the girl's face. His work as service dog helped with some of Abigail's behaviors caused by autism. The girl stopped flapping her hands and stood quietly beside Liam.

Abigail had told no one that William threatened to beat her up if she didn't give him her snowboard. Now she told Liam.

He remembered Mr. Silverbell telling their class that if someone does anything mean, tell a trusted adult.

"Let's tell your mom about William taking your snowboard," Liam advised.

Abigail, Thunder Paws and Liam walked home together. "No one should treat you like that Abigail," Liam told his friend. He took her hand. Abigail pulled it away.

Liam felt sad then remembered Mr. Silverbell explaining to the class that one of the characteristics of autism is not wanting to be touched.

Liam told Abigail's mom about William.

"What a bully William is!" she said, "I'm calling your principal right now!"

Ms. Kazak investigated then summoned William and his mother to her office.

"What's your favorite sport William?" Ms. Kazak asked.

"Hockey."

"How would you feel if someone said they'd hurt you if you didn't give them your hockey stick?"

Williams face became red and his eyes filled with tears.

"I - I'd be scared."

"That's exactly how you've made Abigail feel."

Mrs. Royal stood up "We're going home right now to get Abigail's snowboard!

"Thank you very much for letting me know his shenanigans, Ms. Kazak. We'll be back in an

hour."

"William Harry Royal you have a brand new snowboard. Why did you have to take someone

else's?"

He knew he was in big trouble when his mother used his middle name.

Ten minutes later they reached home.

"Go get Abigail's snowboard right now!"

William went to his bedroom and pulled the snowboard from under the bed.

His mother pointed at William and screamed "You're grounded for a month William Harry!"

William's mother marched her son to the principal's office and gave Ms. Kazak the snowboard.

The principal propped it against her office wall for Abigail.

"Bullying behavior is not allowed. You need to write a letter to Abigail," Ms. Kazak said.

The principal scrutinized the letter very carefully.

The next day she called Abigail and William to her office.

Thunder Paws sat at Abigail's feet.

'Wholely woofin' dog poop,' he thought, 'I smell that Ms. Kazak is very angry.'

"Read the letter William," the principal commanded.

Dear Abigail,

I'm very very sorry. I should not have taken your snowboard. I will never bully you again.

I'm very sorry.

"Very sorry, very sorry, very sorry," Abigail echoed. Thunder Paws thought "Wholely woofin dog poopoop, time for work," as he nudged Abigail's arm and licked the girls face. Abigail then sat quietly on her chair beside William.

Ms. Kazak sat opposite them behind her desk.

"Let's talk about kindness. What could you do to show kindness?"

"I could share my M&M's," William responded.

"I'll pass you the puck when we play hockey," Abigail added.

The principal accompanied them as they returned to class.

Abigail and Thunder Paws sat near Liam. William's desk was adjacent to Mr. Silverbell's.

At recess Abigail said, "Thanks Liam 'cos of you I got my snowboard back. And I'm not afraid of William no more."

Thunder Paws wagged his tail and thought, "Wholely woofin' dog poop. I smell happiness.

Maybe I'll get a treat!"

"Good dog, Thunder Paws," Abigail said as she gave him one from her pocket.

A week later, the entire school was at Mount Werner. It was an annual event sponsored by parents at Abigail's school.

Children's excited voices could be heard. They pointed and shouted,

"Look look! Abigail and Thunder Paws are on one snowboard! I wish my dog could do that!"

At lunchtime Abigail glanced around looking for a place to sit in the crowded lodge.

"Sit beside us!" Four of her classmates yelled.

Abigail and her service dog joined the group.

"Did you see the photographer taking pictures? Where did you learn to shred like that?"

After lunch Abigail and Thunder Paws rode the mountain. Her friends followed. When they reached the base area, most of the school lined the slopes and cheered.

At lunchtime the next day William brought a copy of the newspaper picture with Abigail and Thunder Paws shredding and gave it to Abigail.

"Wholely woofin' dog poop I smell kindness!"

That night as Abigail and Thunder Paws curled up in bed together they happily dreamed of snowboarding fresh powder.

Willam never bullied anyone ever again.

The end

Bibliography

Beane, Allan L. *Together We Can Be Bully Free: A Mini Guide for Parents*. Minneapolis: Free Spirit Publishing, 2011.

Berne, Jennifer. *On a Beam of Light: A Story of Albert Einstein*. San Francisco: Chronicle Books, 2013.

Brown, Don. *Odd Boy Out: Young Albert Einstein*. Boston: Houghton Mifflin, 2004.

Coloroso, Barbara. The Bully, The Bullied, and the Bystander: From Pre-School To High School- How Parents and Teachers Can Help Break The Cycle Of Violence. Toronto: Harper Collins, 2006.

Cook O'Toole, Jennifer. *Sisterhood of the Spectrum: An Asperger Chick's Guide to Life*. London & Philadelphia: Jessica Kingsley, 2015.

Long, Lorie. *A Dog Who's Always Welcome: Assistance and Therapy Dog Trainers Teach You How to Socialize and Train Your Companion Dog*. Hoboken: Wiley, 2008.

Savalox, Heather. "It Takes Courage." *REPS Reaching Everyone Preventing Suicide*, 2 Dec. 2015, 1 Apr. 2019 <http://steamboatsuicideprevention.com/it-takes-courage/>.

Schnurr, Rosina G. *Asperger's Huh? A Child's Perspective*. Ottawa: Anisor Publishing, 2002.

U.S. Department of Education. "U.S. Department of Education Provides Guidance to Help Classroom Teachers Combat Bullying." *Archived Information*. 28 Sept. 2012. 1 Apr. 2019 <https://www.ed.gov/news/press-releases/us-department-education-provides-guidance-helpclassroom-teachers-combat-bullying>.

Printed in the United States
By Bookmasters